CHRISTIAN ZIONISM

A Biblical Response to Confusion, Criticism, and Cultural Pressure

DR. SUSAN MICHAEL

EMBASSY
PUBLISHERS

Christian Zionism: A Biblical Response to Confusion, Criticism, and Cultural Pressure
By Dr. Susan Michael

Email: embassy.publishers@icejusa.org
www.embassypublishers.org

Copyright © 2026 Dr. Susan Michael
Embassy Publishers
PO Box 332974
Murfreesboro, TN 37133-2974

Print ISBN: 979-8-9881386-7-9

For permissions contact: embassy.publishers@icejusa.org
Editorial: Susan Michael; Copyeditor: Karen Engle
Cover design and layout: Peter Ecenroad
Formatting: Nancy Schimp

Printed in the United States of America

■■■ CONTENTS

▥ INTRODUCTION

I n recent years, the term Christian Zionism has gained increased attention and scrutiny due to rising antisemitism seeking to delegitimize Israel and her supporters. Prominent public figures have criticized the historical, biblical, and theological basis that connects Christians to their support of the modern State of Israel.

One media personality even dismissed the movement as a collective "brain virus," suggesting the Christian Zionist conviction is a pathology. Common caricatures suggest that Christian Zionism is a heresy, and adherents put Israel's interests over America's and blindly support the Israeli government no matter what. Some even claim that the Israel of the Bible has nothing to do with modern Israel.

These claims are far from the truth.

This booklet aims to provide clarity amid the confusion and offer biblical grounding for what Christian Zionism is—and is not. When all the rhetoric is stripped away, Christian Zionism, ultimately, asks one simple but fundamental question: *Does God still have a distinct calling for the Jewish people and the land of Israel?* And if He does, the logical next question is: *What does this mean for Christians today?*

Whether the term Christian Zionism is new to you, you are unsure of your position, or you seek a deeper understanding, this booklet was designed for you. My goal is to help you not just understand Christian Zionism better but be able to engage thoughtfully with others about it, balancing conviction with grace and humility.

The hour is late, and it's time to stand firm.

Dr. Susan Michael

ICEJ USA President

CHAPTER 1

WHO ARE CHRISTIAN ZIONISTS?

The term Christian Zionist was first used at the end of the nineteenth century; therefore, it is a relatively new concept and one that requires some explanation. In addition, it is often discussed amid controversy surrounding the highly emotive subject of modern Israel, leading to easy mischaracterization. Defining the term is therefore crucial, and a correct definition must start with an explanation of Zionism itself.

ZIONISM

Zionism today refers to the largely secular political movement that began in the late 1800s and led to the founding of the State of Israel in 1948. Therefore, the term "Christian Zionism" could be considered an oxymoron describing a religious affiliation with a secular movement, which helps explain some of the misunderstanding and debate surrounding it.

Anti-Israel activists have demonized the term Zionism, which has had a detrimental effect on the use of the term Christian Zionism. It is the same with the term Evangelical Christian; anti-Christian liberals have so demonized the word "Evangelical" that, increasingly, Christians are no longer using it.

Personally, I do not want to give up on the term Zionism because it is, at its root, a biblical concept. The word "Zion" denotes Jerusalem, the very place God brought the people He chose for Himself to worship and the center of His redemptive activity. Zion is a real place in Israel, but also a theological symbol of God's faithfulness, kingship, and future restoration: from Zion, God's law will go forth (Isaiah 2:3; Micah 4:2), and from Zion, Jesus will one day rule and reign (Zechariah 14:4; Acts 1:9–12).

Ultimately, Zion (Jerusalem)[1] is the one place on the face of the earth where God chose to set His name and dwell among His people:

> For the Lord has chosen Zion; He has desired it for His dwelling place: "This is My resting place forever; here I will dwell, for I have desired it." (Psalm 132:13–14)

After Rome destroyed Jerusalem in AD 70 and the Jewish people were exiled among the nations, where they have been for over 2,000 years, the hope of returning to Zion became central to Jewish life, prayer, sentiments, and most importantly, identity. Zionism is thus the modern political outworking of thousands of years of Jewish longing to return to Zion.

At its heart, Zionism is a religious movement that needed a political effort to make it a reality. Christian supporters of Israel tend to view Zionism within this biblical context and not as a separate political movement that is somehow distinct and to be disdained. It is a natural progression and a necessary expression of the spiritual love for Zion found in the Bible.

---

1 In the Bible, Zion originally referred to a place: the Jebusite stronghold conquered by David (see 2 Samuel 5:7), a hill in Jerusalem. Over time, the word expanded and took on spiritual meaning, being used poetically and in a theological sense for Jerusalem as a whole.

CHRISTIAN ZIONIST

A definition of Christian Zionist would then be a Christian who supports the right of Jews to self-determination in their ancient homeland. Under this definition, former International Christian Embassy Jerusalem (ICEJ) Executive Director Rev. Malcolm Hedding writes that "many Christians would qualify, no matter what their reasons are for this support."[2]

The term was first used in 1897 at the First Zionist Congress by Theodore Herzl. This father of the Zionist Movement used the term when acknowledging the presence of several Christians among the Congress attendees. One of those Christian Zionists was Jean Henri Dunant, founder of the Red Cross. Those Christians supported the return of the Jews to their homeland for both biblical and moral reasons—it was an act of justice for a persecuted people.

Much has happened since 1897, and today, there are many reasons a Christian should support the return of the Jewish people to their ancient homeland and the modern State of Israel. What follows are a few of the most common, spanning from personal, practical, and political to biblical.[3]

Personal Reasons

Millions of Christians have visited Israel and its holy sites and seen their Bible come alive in profoundly life-transforming ways. It only stands to reason that these pilgrims return with an excitement about Israel and a deep appreciation for the country. They were blessed by the fact that Israel protects their access to sacred places and preserves the archaeological treasures of biblical history found there.

2 Malcolm Hedding, "What Is Christian Zionism?" *Charisma Magazine Online*, 26 Mar. 2010, https://mycharisma.com/news/what-is-christian-zionism2/. Accessed 19 Dec. 2025.

3 For further information, please download "Five Reasons Christians Should Support Israel" at: www.icejusa.org/5-reasons-christians-should-support-israel

Communal Reasons

Christians support Israel because Israel provides the only safe haven for Christians in the Middle East and is consequently the only country in the region in which the Christian community is growing. This Israeli minority enjoys full Israeli citizenship, freedom of worship, and greater opportunities for advancement than in any Muslim country.

Practical Reasons

Israel's incredible contributions across healthcare, agriculture, and technology are saving lives, creating jobs, and enriching communities worldwide. Israel is home to over 1,000 medical device companies and ranks among the world's leading countries in terms of patents per capita. These companies are leading at the intersection of hi-tech and health care and generating cutting-edge devices and medical care used in hospitals around the world.

Political Reasons

Israel is the only liberal democracy in the Middle East and shares our values of freedom of speech, freedom of worship, and human rights. By supporting Israel, America not only helps safeguard democracy in the Middle East but also strengthens its own security and global leadership. We benefit greatly from Israel's intelligence and security expertise.

Economic Reasons

Support of Israel is a good investment. All 50 states in the United States benefit from cooperative agreements with Israel, and out of 250 multinational companies with operations in Israel, 80 percent are US companies. Benefits like this are realized around the world, and the greatest blessing for the Palestinian people lies in an alliance with Israel through which they, too, would enjoy the benefits of her strong economy and free society.

Legal Reasons

Israel's founding was completely legal and formulated by the community of nations as reflected in the 1917 Balfour Declaration, the 1920 San Remo Conference Resolution, the 1922 League of Nations vote, the 1947 UN Partition Plan, and Israel's admission to the United Nations in 1949. Every country in the Middle East was founded out of the same legal process after the end of the Ottoman Empire. Israel's founding was legal, and Christian support is justified.

Moral Reasons

The tragic history of Jewish-Christian relations was plagued by antisemitism perpetuated by confessing Christians. The acknowledgment of this history has moved many Christians today to condemn the demonization of the Jewish people and stand with Israel while seeking ways to establish a new relationship with them based on mutual respect. Their support of Israel is an outgrowth of their desire to make amends and be a blessing to the Jewish people.

Biblical Reasons

The biblical basis for Christian support for Israel is extensive and is not reliant on one isolated section of the Bible but found throughout. Old Testament covenants concerning the calling of the Jewish people and their gift of land beginning in Genesis 12 are affirmed throughout the Psalms, the prophetic books, and the New Testament. God's Word makes it unmistakably clear: we have a biblical mandate to love and bless the people and nation He set apart to bring glory to His name and to fulfill His redemptive plan for the world.

CONCLUSION

One must conclude that while there are many convincing arguments based on history, morality, and common sense to support Israel, for Bible-based Christians, the biblical basis for Christian support of Israel—Christian Zionism—trumps them all and demands our lifelong pursuit of loving and blessing the Jewish people. The next chapter will discuss the biblical basis for supporting Israel in greater detail.

CHAPTER 2

WHAT IS CHRISTIAN ZIONISM?

Christian Zionism is a theological framework based on God's promises to Abraham, confirmed by the Hebrew prophets, and reinforced by the New Testament writings. It is not a new concept and throughout history, it has ebbed and flowed. This means that a narrower use of the term Christian Zionist is one who holds to the theological school of thought known as Christian Zionism and supports the right of the Jewish people to return to their homeland on scriptural grounds.

CHRISTIAN ZIONISM

According to Anglican priest and theologian Gerald McDermott in the book *The New Christian Zionism: Fresh Perspectives on Israel and the Land*, Christian Zionism refers to the belief that the recent gathering of Jews in the land of Israel, and their establishment of a polity there, are fulfillments of biblical prophecy.[4]

Donald Lewis, Phd, former professor of church history at

---

4 Gerald R. McDermott, Ed. *The New Christian Zionism: Fresh Perspectives on Israel and the Land* (Downers Grove, IL: InterVarsity Press, 2016), 12.

Regent College and author of *A Short History of Christian Zionism*, stated that Christian Zionists believe strongly that the State of Israel is ordained by God, a fulfillment of biblical prophecy, and "solid evidence of God's direct intervention in history."[5] Lewis defined Christian Zionism across time as "a Christian movement that holds to the belief that the Jewish people have a biblically mandated claim to their ancient homeland in the Middle East."[6]

THE OLD TESTAMENT

The key tenants of Christian Zionism are found in Genesis 12:1–3, where God promised Abraham a great nation of descendants, a land, and a mission to bless the world:

> Now the LORD had said to Abram: "Get out of your country, from your family and from your father's house, to a land that I will show you. I will make you a great nation; I will bless you and make your name great; and you shall be a blessing. I will bless those who bless you, and I will curse him who curses you; and in you all the families of the earth shall be blessed." (Genesis 12:1–3)

Hedding writes: "The biblical foundation for Christian Zionism is found in God's covenant with Abraham. It was in this covenant that God chose Abraham to birth a nation through which He would redeem the world, and to do this, He bequeathed them a land on which to exist as His chosen nation."[7]

Genesis 17 establishes that the covenant God made with Abraham was everlasting; therefore, the gift of the land was everlasting:

---

5 Donald M. Lewis, *A Short History of Christian Zionism: From the Reformation to the Twenty-First Century* (Downers Grove, IL: InterVarsity Press, 2021), 243.

6 Lewis, *A Short History*, 3.

7 Hedding, "What Is Christian Zionism?" *MyCharisma.com*.

And I will establish My covenant between Me and you and your descendants after you in their generations, for an everlasting covenant, to be God to you and your descendants after you. Also I give to you and your descendants after you the land in which you are a stranger, all the land of Canaan, as an everlasting possession; and I will be their God. (Genesis 17:7–8)

The later Mosaic covenant stipulated that the right to live on the land promised to them would be determined by their obedience to God's instruction and their relationship with Him. Sin and disobedience would result in Israel's exile from the land for a season, but exile never annulled the promise. Whether the children of Israel were in or out of the land, the land remained theirs by divine covenant, granted by God and never revoked.

The Hebrew prophets proclaimed the arrival of judgment and punishment for sin, as well as a future restoration to their land and to their God. Christian Zionism recognizes God's hand in the return of the Jewish people to their ancient homeland after 2,000 years of exile and rejoices in God's faithfulness to His promises.

THE NEW TESTAMENT

The New Testament was written by Second Temple–period Jews who clearly understood God's promises to their people and were awaiting their fulfillment. They interpreted the ministry, death, and resurrection of Jesus within the context of those promises, not as a replacement of them.

This is evident in the disciples' final conversation with the resurrected Jesus before His ascension into heaven when they asked, "Lord, will You at this time restore the kingdom to Israel?" (Acts 1:6). Jesus' response did not deny that future event— He simply responded, "It is not for you to know times or seasons which the Father has put in His own authority" (v. 7).

The apostle Paul, therefore, wrote in Romans 11 that even though the majority of the Jewish people had not accepted Jesus' messianic credentials, the promises to them were still valid. The promise of a universal mission and the gift of land found in the Abrahamic promise remained:

> Concerning the gospel they are enemies for your sake, but concerning the election they are beloved for the sake of the fathers. For the gifts and the calling of God are irrevocable. (vv. 28–29)

CONCLUSION

Christian Zionism is, therefore, the belief that God bequeathed the land to the Jewish people as an everlasting possession for the purposes of world redemption. This is the biblical foundation for Christian support for Israel and the Jewish people.

CHAPTER 3

ISRAEL IN THE NEW TESTAMENT

The Christian reader may have several questions at this point concerning Israel in the New Testament. So let's take a brief look at some key verses and recommended resources for further study.

The first resource that everyone must read is Gerald McDermott's *Israel Matters*. In this book, McDermott shares his personal journey from supersessionism to Christian Zionism. His chapter on the New Testament is a great place for those seeking a better understanding to start. For readers ready to dig deeper into the topic, McDermott's book *The New Christian Zionism* offers a more thorough and academic discussion of the subject. For the purposes of this booklet, here are a few thoughts to encourage further study.

VALIDITY OF OLD TESTAMENT PROMISES

Replacement theologians often emphasize that the Old Testament and Judaism have been brought to an end and were replaced with something totally and completely new—Christianity. But this is precisely the approach Paul warned against in Romans 11, when he refers to the root of Christianity as being

Jewish and warns against an arrogant position that does not honor the root. According to McDermott, "For Paul, then, the believing church will never be separated from its root, Jewish Israel. If the church thinks it can be separate and in fact replace Jewish Israel, it has become 'proud' and 'arrogant.'"[8]

A popular type of Replacement Theology is Fulfillment Theology, which teaches that Jesus fulfilled the Law, so it is no longer relevant. However, Jesus said: "Do not think that I came to destroy the Law or the Prophets. I did not come to destroy but to fulfill" (Matthew 5:17). Some say even the Ten Commandments do not apply to Christians because Jesus brought a new set of ethics, when, in fact, in His Sermon on the Mount, Jesus expounded upon the basic principles found of the Ten Commandments—He did not replace them with something new.

THE PROMISED LAND

The God of the Bible is the God of the whole earth. Yet His promise of this piece of land to one family—the descendants of Abraham, through Isaac and then Jacob—is confirmed and repeated in Scripture 46 times. Clearly, this attention affirms the importance of the land in God's purposes. Land is a necessary element for forming a nation.

The land also provided a stage on which the Almighty God carried out His plan of redemption. As long as God's covenant with Abraham was in play (everlasting), the land belonged to his descendants (everlasting). The land is an integral part of the covenant because it is the place where God would work through His people and fulfill His promise to bless the world. But does the New Testament even mention the land?

Indeed, it does! However, one problem Christian Bible readers face is the English translation of a Greek word that can mean "land" or "earth." For example, Matthew 5:5 states, "Blessed are the meek, for they shall inherit the *earth*" (emphasis added).

---

8 Gerald R. McDermott, *Israel Matters* (Grand Rapids, MI: Brazos Press, 2017), 29.

Many scholars are beginning to recognize that a better translation is "Blessed are the meek, for they shall inherit the *land*." This is more in keeping with the Jewish context of inheriting the land of Israel as reflected in Psalm 37.

As discussed in chapter 2, Jesus did not deny that there would be a future Israel [in the land] when asked in Acts 1:6–7. Paul predicted that one day "all Israel will be saved" because Israel's deliverer would "come out of Zion" (Romans 11:26), and Peter referred to the "restoration of all things" in Acts 3:21, which was a Greek term based on the Old Testament concept of the future return of the Jews to the land and reestablishment of a Jewish nation.[9]

THE RETURN OF JEWS TO THE LAND

Though some argue the prophecies of Israel's return were fulfilled when Jews returned to rebuild Jerusalem after the Babylonian captivity, this does not align with Jesus' very teachings, and what His disciples believed, about a future for Israel.

Jesus prophesied a coming exile of the Jewish people and Gentile control of Jerusalem, but only for a time. Gentile rule would come to an end one day, and Jerusalem would come under Jewish control: "And they will fall by the edge of the sword and be led away captive into all nations. And Jerusalem will be *trampled* by Gentiles until the times of the Gentiles are fulfilled" (Luke 21:24, emphasis added). It is important to note that Gentiles indeed controlled Jerusalem for the next 1,900 years until it came under Israeli sovereignty in 1967.

THE RETURN OF JESUS TO JERUSALEM

In His Olivet Discourse, Jesus looked over the city of Jerusalem and prophesied the coming destruction of the city and the temple. But he also prophesied in Luke 13:35 that one day, the Jewish people would welcome Him back to the city with the

---

9 McDermott, *Israel Matters*, 30.

Hebrew greeting *Baruch Haba BaShem Adonai* ("Blessed is He who comes in the name of the Lord"). *Jesus would return to a Jewish Jerusalem.*

In Matthew 19 Jesus speaks of reigning from His throne in the New Jerusalem, judging the 12 tribes of Israel (v. 28). McDermott, citing Markus Bockmuehl, says indications in the Gospels seem to affirm "the early Jesus movement . . . continued to focus upon the restoration of Israel's 12 tribes in a new, messianic kingdom."[10] In Mark 11:17, Jesus quoted Isaiah's prophecy concerning a restored Jerusalem. Each of these prophecies speaks of a literal, physical place from where Jesus will one day rule and reign.

THE NEW JERUSALEM

The book of Revelation also affirms that Israel, as a particular land, has a place in God's plan for the future. McDermott observes: "Christians are right to say that the Bible speaks of the whole earth being renewed. But not all Christians have seen that the center of the renewed earth will be Israel."[11]

The Bible depicts the Lamb standing on Mount Zion (Revelation 14:1), the new earth that is to come centered in Jerusalem, and the New Jerusalem adorned with 12 gates inscribed with the "twelve tribes of the sons of Israel" (Revelation 21:2, 12).

CONCLUSION

Clearly, the New Testament carries on the Old Testament principle of the importance of the land and reaffirms the covenants, the law, and the prophetic writings, all of which point to a future return of the Jews to the land and a coming glorious day when the kingdom of God is on earth.

---

10 Gerald McDermott, Ed., *The New Christian Zionism: Fresh Perspectives on Israel and the Land* (IVEP Academic, 2016), citing Markus Bockmuehl, *Jewish Law in Gentile Churches: Halakhah and the Beginning of Christian Public Ethics*, Baker Academic, 2000, p. xi.

11 McDermott, *Israel Matters*, 30–31.

⊓⊔

CHAPTER 4

HISTORICAL ORIGINS OF CHRISTIAN ZIONISM

Christian Zionism is not a modern invention. While the term is relatively new, its roots stretch back centuries—in fact, as far back as the early church.

Just as Jesus and the disciples were Jewish, so were almost all of the New Testament authors, as was the early church they wrote about. As a result of their deep understanding of the Hebrew Scriptures, these authors believed in the everlasting validity of the Abrahamic covenant. They also believed in the literal accuracy of the prophecies regarding the life and ministry of Jesus as well as those about future events, including the restoration of a kingdom to Israel.[12]

In the first century, church fathers still held to the theological expectation of a restored nation of Israel. Dr. Tricia Miller, director of CAMERA's Partnership of Christians and Jews, writes:

> The expectation of a future return of the Jewish people to the land and the restoration of the nation of Israel was also fairly common in the early church. Tertullian, a third-century leader, said: "It will be fitting for

12 See McDermott, *The New Christian Zionism*, pp. 52–54.

the Christian to rejoice, and not to grieve, at the restoration of Israel, if it be true, as it is, that the whole of our hope is intimately united with the remaining expectation of Israel."[13]

As the church grew over time, it became predominantly Gentile. Christians—from pagan backgrounds with little knowledge of the Hebrew Scriptures—lost sight of the Jewish roots of their faith and God's promises to the Jewish people. Most did not even know that Jesus was Jewish.

THE COUNCIL OF NICAEA

The Council of Nicaea of AD 325 was a turning point in that separation. This Council was monumental in affirming the divine nature of Jesus, articulated most clearly in what became known as the Nicene Creed. In his article "Healing the Rift: 1700 Years After the Nicaea Council," ICEJ President Dr. Juergen Buehler states: "While the creed and the 20 canons that emerged from Nicaea were free of anti-Jewish rhetoric, the official letters [to distribute the creed to churches throughout the world] from Emperor Constantine contained a critical and condescending attitude toward the Jews."[14] This tone spread throughout the church, resulting in anti-Jewish preaching by some of the most notable church fathers.

NICAEA TO THE REFORMATION

For well over 1,000 years, most of the church believed that Christians had replaced the Jews as the people of God's covenant. Known as Replacement Theology, this interpretive framework

---

13 Tricia Miller, PhD, CAMERA, "No, Tucker, Christian Zionism is NOT Christian Heresy! *Israel365News*, November 5, 2025, https://israel365news.com/413777/no-tucker-christian-zionism-is-not-christian-heresy.

14 Juergen Buehler, "Healing the Rift: 1700 Years After the Nicaea Council," *ICEJ USA*, May 17, 2025, https://icejusa.org/2025/05/17/healing-the-rift-1700-years-after-the-nicaea-council/.

reads the Scriptures allegorically. God's promises to the Jewish people are spiritualized and applied to the church. In rare instances, monks and priests read the Scriptures differently; however, in the church's first thousand years, this view remained predominant and became the fuel that fed centuries of Christian antisemitism.

THE REFORMATION

This began to change in the fifteenth and sixteenth centuries when the Bible was translated into the languages of the common people, including into English. Christians began reading Scripture for themselves. They learned about Christianity's Jewish roots and the promised return of the Jews to their ancient homeland.

As a result, respected theologians and preachers taught of a future Jewish restoration to the land of Israel. Entire movements of Christians began praying for this return. By the eighteenth century, the Restorationist movement had blossomed and included many theologians, writers, and politicians. This movement continued to grow in the nineteenth century; the term "Christian Zionist" was first used by Theodore Herzl, who acknowledged the participation of some key Christian supporters at the first Zionist Congress in 1897. Christian leaders had expanded their involvement in the Zionist cause beyond prayer to advocacy. They did all that they could to help the Jewish people return to Israel.

Christian Zionists today are proud to follow in the footsteps of a multitude of Bible-believers from numerous theological persuasions, countries, and professions—men and women who saw overwhelming evidence in Scripture for God's continuing covenant with the Jewish people and their right to their ancient homeland. While many Christian Zionists today may differ with these pioneers on other points of theology or politics, they all agree on the biblical significance of the restoration of Israel.[15]

---

15 For further information on some of the most notable members of this movement throughout the ages, go to: www.israelanswers.com/page/christian_zionist_hall_of_fame.

CONCLUSION

From the early church fathers through the Reformation and beyond, a faithful remnant of believers has stood firm in their conviction that God's covenant with the Jewish people—His promise to be an everlasting people and a blessing to the world in a specific land—remains unbroken. And though Replacement Theology caused a centuries-long schism between the church and synagogue, the modern shift away from it[16] has enabled the church to rediscover its Jewish roots and recognize Israel's restoration—both physical (to the land) and a future spiritual restoration.

Clearly, Christian support for the Jewish people did not originate in 1948 with the birth of the State of Israel. Instead, deep-rooted biblical conviction is the driving force behind the Zionist vision. With this historical foundation, let's now turn to the biblical and legal rights governing the relationship between the Jewish people and the land.

---

16 Juergen Buehler, "Israel and the Church: A Coming Reformation," ICEJ USA, September 24, 2024, https://icejusa.org/2024/09/24/israel-and-the-church-a-coming-reformation/.

CHAPTER 5

WHAT CHRISTIAN ZIONISM IS NOT

O ver time, efforts to delegitimize Israel have also attempted to discredit Christian Zionism. Opponents have claimed it is a new movement that is a politicalization of Scripture, heretical, and is only about Armageddon. The Jewish community has been told the movement has ulterior motives and cannot be trusted. It is important to unpack a few of these false claims and clarify, as McDermott says, what Christian Zionism *is not*.[17]

DISPENSATIONALISM

Dispensationalism is a theology originating in the nineteenth century by Nelson Darby and made popular through the notes of the Scofield version of the King James Bible. It puts Israel and the church on two different tracks throughout history with an elaborate scheme of end-time events. While dispensationalists are pro-Israel, most Christian Zionists today do not adhere to this interpretation of Scripture.

Christian Zionism does not hold to such a specific schedule of dispensations or end-time events and predates Dispensationalism by about 18 centuries![18]

---

17 McDermott, *The New Christian Zionism*, 15–24.
18 McDermott, *The New Christian Zionism*, 15.

A PUSH FOR AN END-TIME SCENARIO

Christian Zionism is not based on prophecy and should not be seen as an attempt to accelerate an apocalyptic timeline. Christian Zionism is based on God's promises—those spoken to Abraham, made part of the Mosaic covenant, then confirmed by the Hebrew prophets. While the prophecies will most certainly come to pass, predicting how they will occur involves a good degree of speculation.

The firm foundation of Christian Zionism is the very promises of God found in His covenants with Israel[19] and His faithfulness to fulfill those promises.

HERESY

The accusation that Christian Zionism is a heresy recently went viral when spoken by a well-known media personality who had only recently read the Bible for the first time and obviously did not know much Christian history as well. Some of the greatest and most respected Evangelicals in history were what might today be called Christian Zionists: John and Charles Wesley, Charles Haddon Spurgeon, Bishop Ryle of Liverpool, Professor Jacob Janeway of the Scottish National Church, and many others. The only difference between them and today's Christian Zionists is that they looked forward in hope to a future event; today's Christian Zionists—numbering in the hundreds of millions—have witnessed the return of the Jews to their homeland and actively support a current reality.[20]

---

19 Malcolm Hedding, "*The Great Covenants of the Bible*," Biblical Zionism Study Series, International Christian Embassy Jerusalem, 48.

20 Susan Michael, "Warning Christians about Antisemitism," *ICEJ USA*, February 9, 2023, https://icejusa.org/2023/02/09/warning-christians-about-antisemitism/

NATIONALISM

Some detractors claim that Zionism is just one of many nationalist movements of the late eighteenth and nineteenth centuries. Though the Zionist movement did benefit from this wave of nationalism, it long predated it.[21] Christian Zionism views the Zionist movement of the late eighteenth century as a necessary political effort to realize the return of the Jewish people to Zion in fulfillment of God's plans and purposes. He is sovereign and used nationalism to fulfill the longing to return to Zion, evident in the daily prayers of the Jewish people throughout their 2,000 years of exile.

It is also important to note that not all Jews were in exile, and generations have lived in the land of Israel for 3,000 years. Zionism is deeply connected to ancient, divine land promises, a consistent Jewish presence in the land, and centuries of Jewish longing to return home for those living outside it.

CONDONING STOLEN LAND

Israel's detractors have tried to rewrite history in such a way that Israel is a colonialist aggressor founded on stolen land. If that were true, then Christians would be guilty of supporting theft of land.[22] It is important to establish that these claims are false. Though Jewish connection to the land spans some 4,000 years, modern Jewish immigration to then Palestine[23] began with land

---

21 McDermott, *The New Christian Zionism*, 15.
22 McDermott, *The New Christian Zionism*, 20–21.
23 The term Palestine derives from the Hebrew *Pelesheth* ("land of the Philistines"), referencing Israel's ancient enemies. After the Bar Kokhba revolt in the second century CE, the Romans renamed the province Syria Palaestina to diminish Jewish national identity and replace the name Judaea. The region was referred to as Palestine under successive empires, including Ottoman rule until 1917 and British administration under the League of Nations Mandate (1922–1948), but no sovereign state of Palestine has ever existed. In 1947, the United Nations proposed partitioning the territory into Jewish and Arab states; Jewish leaders accepted the plan, while Arab leaders rejected it. Today, the Palestinian Authority exercises limited self-governance in parts of Judea and Samaria (AKA the West

purchases there in the late nineteenth and early twentieth centuries and the creation of agricultural communities. When Israel declared independence in 1948, there was a transfer of public lands previously held by the British Mandate.

The new Israeli government invited Arabs living inside its borders to remain as citizens. However, the surrounding Arab nations responded by declaring war on the infant nation, displacing hundreds of thousands of Arabs and Jews. But Arab states failed to absorb the Palestinian Arab refugees, while Israel absorbed the Jewish refugees expelled from Arab nations. Vacated Arab properties were absorbed by Israel, just as vacated Jewish properties were absorbed by the Arab countries in which they had resided. While some grievances do exist, the overwhelming historical, legal, and demographic evidence affirms that Israel's establishment was lawful and legitimate.[24]

RACIST

Another tactic Israel's enemies use is to blame the Jewish State for being racist. Nothing could be further from the truth, but due to the effectiveness of this campaign, we must address it, or else Christian Zionism could be considered racist as well. When it comes to Israel's treatment of the Arab people, one need only look to its Arab citizens to see that Israel is clearly not a racist state. The charge of apartheid (racial segregation) is based on the previous dismantling of the real apartheid regime in South Africa in the mid-90s; it is being used to isolate Israel internationally and bring about her demise through boycotts, divestments, and sanctions (BDS).[25]

Bank), and until Israel's 2023–25 war with Hamas, Gaza was completely controlled by Hamas.

24 Susan Michael, "Was Israel Founded on Stolen Land?" *ICEJ USA*, April 5, 2022, https://icejusa.org/2022/04/05/was-israel-founded-on-stolen-arab-land/.

25 Susan Michael, "Is Israel an Apartheid State?" *ICEJ USA*, April 12, 2022, https://icejusa.org/2022/04/12/is-israel-a-racist-apartheid-state/.

ANTI-ARAB

Another accusation thrown at Christian Zionists is one of being anti-Arab, whereas Christians should love all people. A Christian approach to the Arab-Israeli conflict must be one not only grounded in love for all the people involved, but one that is biblically founded and discerns between what is historical fact and politically motivated mistruths. One will then understand that the greatest blessing for the Arab people is found in God's covenant with the people of Israel. It is because of God's love for the world that He brought into existence the nation of Israel through whom He would bring about His plan to redeem that world. His intention was not to bless the Jewish people to the exclusion of the rest of the world, but that through them, He would "bless all the families of the earth" (Genesis 12:3).[26]

Therefore, it is absolutely pro-Arab to be pro-Israel.

ENCOURAGING INJUSTICE

The issue of justice is critical. Israel is required to treat aliens in the land well and not to oppress them (Exodus 22:21). If Israel is guilty of oppression or injustice, then her Christian supporters would be guilty of encouraging sin. So let's look at Israel's treatment of aliens, starting with the 2 million Arabs living in Israel. They have citizenship, can vote (including women), have freedom of speech, have their own political parties, serve in the Knesset, serve on the Supreme Court, and can even be "Miss Israel." Israel is the only country in the whole Middle East in which the Christian Arab population is growing. *Why aren't the Christian Arabs fleeing Israel like they are the Muslim world?* Obviously, they have found more justice in Israel than in any of the Arab countries. That seems like pretty convincing proof that

---

26 Susan Michael, "Is It Anti-Arab to be Pro-Israel?" *ICEJ USA*, September 20, 2016, https://icejusa.org/2016/09/20/is-it-anti-arab-to-be-pro-israel/.

Israel is not an unjust or repressive country.[27]

The Palestinian people living in Judea and Samaria (also called the West Bank) under the Palestinian Authority and in Gaza under Hamas do have more difficult circumstances and do not have the freedom of movement necessary to develop businesses, find jobs, or even get to a hospital sometimes. But to blame Israel for the tight borders and checkpoints without ever mentioning why they are needed is disingenuous.

The real culprits here are the corrupt Palestinian leaders who have not only filled their own bank accounts instead of bettering the people's lives but have refused to sit down at the negotiating table and hammer out a better life for their people. This is because of their Islamic ideology—not Zionism.[28]

CONCLUSION

Many criticisms of Christian Zionism are based on misunderstandings, which, unfortunately, often give rise to misleading narratives that distort biblical truth and harm the global Jewish community. Christian Zionism is not a newer, heretical movement, nor is it motivated by political opportunism or hostility toward Arabs. Christian Zionism seeks justice and loves all people—recognizing that blessing Israel is part of God's broader plan to bring redemption to the world.

For this reason, all Christians must separate fact from fiction and understand what Christian Zionism is not so they can accurately convey its true beliefs and intentions to others.

---

27 "An Open Letter to America's Christian Zionists," ICEJ USA, October 5, 2011, https://icejusa.org/2011/10/05/an-open-letter-to-americas-christian-zionists/

28 "An Open Letter," https://icejusa.org/2011/10/05/an-open-letter-to-americas-christian-zionists/

CHAPTER 6

THEOLOGICAL CHALLENGES AND CONSIDERATIONS

The heart of the divide in the Christian world toward Israel usually comes down to a person's view of the Jewish people's calling and destiny.[29] It may masquerade as a concern for the Palestinian people, or purport to be about political issues, but often the real issue lies in whether they believe in a form of Replacement Theology or not.

REPLACEMENT THEOLOGY

Let's unpack this belief further. Replacement Theology, or supersessionism, is a centuries-old teaching[30] that the Jewish people have been cursed and rejected by God because they rejected Jesus' messianic credentials. As a result, they have been replaced by the church; the church is therefore the new Israel of God. While God's curses may be upon the Jews, His blessings all reside on the church!

---

29 Susan Michael, "Across the Israel Divide," *ICEJ USA*, September 19, 2016, https://icejusa.org/2016/09/19/across-the-israel-divide/.

30 For a concise history of supersessionism and Christian Zionism, see *Israel Matters* by Gerald R. McDermott.

This theology provided fertile ground for centuries of antisemitic teachings in the church and sowed the seeds for the persecution of the Jewish people throughout Europe. Many scholars agree that the Holocaust could never have happened had it not been for the centuries of Christian antisemitism that were rooted in this theology.

Replacement Theology, in all its variations, implies that God's Plan A failed, so He went to Plan B with a new people: the Christian Church. However, Ephesians 1:4–5 says that Plan A existed before the foundations of the world were laid and always included the death of Christ Jesus because that is how Gentile believers are adopted as sons (v. 5). Paul in Romans 11 affirms that the calling of the Jewish people is irrevocable (Romans 11:29). *Plan A did not fail and was not annulled.*

The danger is that if someone believes the Jewish people were so wicked that they lost their covenant with God, that person becomes susceptible to antisemitic lies, which can quickly take root. Proof of this connection is that often, accusations against Israel then morph into derogatory comments about Jews in general, and all is justified by repeating a Replacement Theology position. Replacement Theology opens the door to and provides fertile ground for antisemitism.

CALLING OF THE JEWISH PEOPLE

Christian Zionism, however, is a protective wall against antisemitism because it produces gratitude and respect for the Jewish people. The land of Canaan was bequeathed to them as an everlasting possession for the purposes of becoming a great nation and blessing all the families of the earth (Genesis 12:1–3). They would do this by bringing to a fallen world the redemptive gifts through which man can be saved. The apostle Paul listed those redemptive gifts in Romans 3:2 and Romans 9:4–5: the Word of God, the covenants, the law, the service of God, the promises, and Christ Jesus. The Jewish people's work is not yet complete, and God has brought them back to the land for what may now be the final chapter of history, which is a glorious one, when the knowledge of the Lord will fill the earth and nations will learn war no more (Isaiah 2, 11).

Acknowledging this special calling on the Jewish people entails a responsibility to appreciate, bless, and honor them. However, this does not mean that God loves them above all the other peoples of the world. John 3:16 declares God's love extends to the whole world: "For God so loved the world that He gave His only begotten Son, that whosoever believes in Him should not perish, but have everlasting life."

God's love for the world is why He brought into existence the nation of Israel through whom He would bring about His great plan of redemption. Their role in His plan would afford them a place of preservation and promised blessing. Unfortunately, their calling would also place them directly in the line of fire, and consequently, there would be much suffering throughout the centuries because of it. The story of the Jewish people is filled with exiles, persecutions, pogroms, expulsions, and threats of annihilation. There is no explanation for this history other than the biblical role bequeathed to them by God Himself and the evil battle against it.

Psalm 83:1–4 explains that they are in the line of fire in a war against God Himself: "O God . . . those who hate you . . . have said 'Come, and let us cut them off from being a nation, that the name of Israel may be remembered no more.'" God knew that the people of Israel would pay a price and their history would be full of suffering. This could explain why He promised blessings on any who would bless and help them.

TESTING THE NATIONS

George Gilder, a venture-capitalist, proposes in his book *The Israel Test* that Israel presents a moral and ethical challenge to the world and therefore has become the ultimate fault line. At the root of the Israel test for the world today is the knowledge that Israel is contributing more to humanity through its scientific, technological, and economic achievements than nearly any other country in the world.

According to Gilder, Israel presents the following test to the world: *What is your attitude toward people who surpass you in creating wealth or in other accomplishments? Do you aspire to their excellence, or do you seethe at it? Do you admire and celebrate exceptional achievement, or do you impugn it and seek to tear it down?*

God is using Israel to test the hearts of the nations. Their future will be determined by how they respond.

In Isaiah 11, the return of the Jewish people to their homeland is described as God's banner to the nations. God is declaring a message to the world in this miraculous return—that God's word is true, and He is faithful to fulfill it. This is a message that Christians should rejoice in and rally behind. But the flip side of that message is a clear warning that judgment is coming, and it will be based on their failure of the "Israel test." His word says[31] those who oppose His people and seek to destroy them will be destroyed. It is a clear word of warning.

TESTING THE CHURCH

The same test is being presented to the church. In Romans 11, the apostle Paul addresses the attitude of the Roman church toward the Jewish people. He warns believers to make sure that their attitude is humble and honors the Jewish people. He even cautions them about possible judgment by God if their attitude is not right: "Do not be haughty, but fear. For if God did not spare the natural branches, He may not spare you either" (Romans 11:20–21).

This is the test that Israel presents to the church: *Are we arrogant toward the Jews? Do we seek to replace them in advancing God's will—or do we rejoice in the faithfulness of God to them and*

---

31   Jeremiah 30:11; Joel 3:1–3; Zephaniah 3:19; Zechariah 12:9

that He is fulfilling the promises He made to their fathers? Do we despise their return to their homeland because it does not fit into our Replacement Theology—or do we break into praise of God's mighty ways as did the apostle Paul when he completed his teaching about God's enduring plans for Israel in Romans 9–11?

A church that honors its Hebraic roots, as wild branches that are grafted into the natural olive tree (Romans 11:17), receives great strength and nourishment. Separating ourselves from the very root that supports our Christian faith brings spiritual decline and even death. Christianity has no meaning when separated from its Jewish context. This may explain the decline in certain denominations that belittle the biblical and Hebraic foundation of our faith.

May we all pass this test and approach the issue of Israel and the Jewish people with humility and honor for the spiritual root that supports the Christian faith.

THE CHARACTER OF GOD

The great scandal of Replacement Theology is its assault on the character of God and His faithfulness. The idea that God rejected the Jewish people and took away their promises, giving them to another people—the church—cannot be reconciled with Scripture. If God's plan A failed and He had to come up with a new people to execute plan B, it brings into question His sovereignty and wisdom. *What kind of God has a plan that fails?*

Instead, the reading of Scripture is clear that God's promises to Abraham were not conditional on actions by Abraham or any of his descendants. Genesis 15 reveals that the covenant was not even made with Abraham—it was as though God was making the covenant with Himself. He was the responsible party to fulfill the covenant. So to say that it failed means *He* failed and brings God's character into question.

Scripture is also clear that God is a faithful God: "God is not man, that he should lie, or a son of man, that he should change his mind. Has he said, and will he not do it? Or has he spoken, and will he not fulfill it?" (Numbers 23:19 ESV).

A powerful declaration of God's commitment to His promises is found in Psalm 89:34: "My covenant I will not break." And in the New Testament Timothy says: "If we are faithless, He remains faithful, for He cannot deny Himself" (2 Timothy 2:13).

God is faithful and is fulfilling the promises He made 4,000 years ago to the descendants of Abraham, Isaac, and Jacob. That realization should bring great encouragement to all Christians that He will also fulfill His promises made to us.

CONCLUSION

So if ever you are in a time of discouragement or doubt, remember the return of the Jewish people to the land God promised to Abraham, exactly as foretold by the Hebrew prophets thousands of years ago. We can find hope in this amazing demonstration of the faithfulness of God.

ı.ı

ANTISEMITISM, ISRAEL, AND CHRISTIAN ZIONISM

One cannot address the controversy surrounding Christian Zionism without a discussion about the role antisemitism plays in it. Antisemitism is surging around the world and is not only a threat to the Jewish people—it poses a grave danger to the church as well. While many Christians active in supporting Israel may not fully realize it, we are living in a pivotal moment in history. Antisemitism is not only attempting to demonize Israel and the Jewish people, but also Christians who support them.

ANTISEMITISM

Sadly, for centuries, Christian theology played a role in fostering widespread hostility toward Jews. This deep-rooted enmity embedded in European Christian history gave rise to discrimination, expulsions, and even violence against Jewish communities. Nazism followed with racial antisemitism and sought to rid the human race of the inferior Jews. Antisemitism, however, is not merely a relic of the past—it persists in new forms. Like a virus, it mutates to fit the ideologies of each new generation.

DEMONIZATION OF ISRAEL

While the church has made great progress in turning from that history,[32] antisemitism is resurging—this time in more subtle forms. Political antisemitism—often called anti-Zionism—targets the Jewish collective—the State of Israel. Though not all criticism of Israeli policy is antisemitic, the line is crossed when such criticism denies Israel's right to exist, uses antisemitic rhetoric, or applies double standards not expected of other nations.

This demonization of the Jewish State inevitably leads to attacks on Jews around the world. When Israeli military actions prompt assaults on Jewish individuals in other countries, the connection is clear: this is not political disagreement—it is antisemitism, and the church should take note.

A WARNING TO CHRISTIANS

Antisemitism not only threatens the Jewish people—it aims to sever Christians from their own spiritual roots. As the apostle Paul wrote in Romans 11, the Jewish people are the root that supports the church, and to be cut off from that root is to suffer spiritual death. This is why antisemitism must be recognized as an urgent threat within the church. It robs believers of the foundation of their faith and seeks to disconnect them from the very people who are proof of God's faithfulness. Churches must be vigilant, biblically grounded, and proactive in resisting this evil ideology.

EVIL FORCES BEHIND ANTISEMITISM

At its core, antisemitism is a spiritual attack on God's covenant people. As Psalm 83 says, those who hate God seek to "cut them [Israel] off from being a nation," aiming to erase the name of Israel from memory. The church must recognize this as a spiritual battle and respond accordingly.

---

32   Susan Michael, *Antisemitism: What Every Christian Needs to Know and How to Counter it* (Embassy Publishers, 2023), 20–21.

Revelation 12 portrays this battle using vivid imagery. Israel is a pregnant woman crowned with the sun, the moon, and 12 stars. Sitting before her is an evil dragon, waiting to devour the male Child (Messiah) she will give birth to. But as soon as the Child is delivered, He is caught up into heaven, and the woman is taken into a place of protection. Enraged, the dragon persecutes the woman, yet she remains protected, so he turns to go after her "other offspring"—those who bear the testimony of Jesus. The point is that the same evil forces that hate the woman because of her role in birthing the male Child also hate those who are His followers.

Antisemitism is an evil force that seeks to destroy the Jewish people because, in so doing, the redemptive plan of God will collapse. This same force will also come after those of us who are blessing and supporting the Jewish people and will seek to not only cut us off from our Jewish roots but stop us from proclaiming the good news of the male Child—Jesus.

PROLIFERATION OF LIES

Amid the story in Revelation 12 is found one of the names of the evil dragon that is pursuing the woman and her offspring: "accuser of our brethren" (v. 10). This explains the proliferation of lies and false accusations against Israel, the Jewish people, Zionism, and Christian Zionism. These false accusations are all part of the spiritual battle against God and His plan to destroy evil and redeem this fallen world.

CONCLUSION

We must take a stand. Silence in the face of this vile and growing hostility toward God's people is not an option. *We are in this together!* Now is the time to pray, but also to raise our voices and stand boldly with the State of Israel and the Jewish people. The stakes are high, and the situation is critical. More information about getting involved follows in our final chapter.

■ ■ ■

CHAPTER 8

THE CHRISTIAN ZIONIST MOVEMENT TODAY

The birth of the State of Israel on May 14, 1948, ushered in a new era for Christian Zionism and signaled the late hour on God's time clock. Evangelical Christians became increasingly interested in events in the Middle East and soon began visiting the Holy Land. As Christian tourism increased, so did Christian support for Israel—and Jewish-Christian relations.

1980 – BIRTH OF A MOVEMENT

Notable Christian leaders had become part of Israel's story as discussed in chapter 4. But in 1980, the first global organization was founded in the heart of the newborn State of Israel—the International Christian Embassy Jerusalem (ICEJ). The ICEJ was launched when all embassies moved out of Jerusalem in protest of the city being the capital of Israel. As governments withdrew, Christians from around the world responded by establishing a permanent Christian presence in the city. Today, from its base in Jerusalem, with a reach into more than 180 countries and representation in 90, the ICEJ has translated conviction into action on a global scale.

The ICEJ's mission is to demonstrate Christian support to the people of Israel through practical assistance and partnership. The organization has assisted more than 193,000 Jews in making Aliyah (immigrating to Israel), provided millions of dollars annually in humanitarian aid, and helped build critical infrastructure, including bomb shelters, trauma centers, and assisted living facilities for Holocaust Survivors. The ICEJ has also delivered emergency assistance following wars, terror attacks, and natural disasters while mobilizing Christian advocacy worldwide.

Today, the ICEJ is the largest Christian Zionist organization and a respected pioneer and thought leader for the wider movement.

UNITED STATES OF AMERICA

In the United States, the International Christian Embassy Jerusalem's USA Branch (ICEJ USA) has excelled in the production of educational resources for the Christian community, has been a pioneer in Jewish-Christian relations, and is recognized as a leader of leaders in the American Christian arena.

This leadership is evident in the ICEJ USA's network of leaders—the American Christian Leaders for Israel (ACLI). Founded in 2015 amid mounting concern over Iran's nuclear ambitions and escalating threats to Israel, ACLI began with just a dozen leaders. It has since grown into a national network capable of mobilizing rapidly and speaking with unity during moments of crisis by leveraging Christian voices across media, grassroots advocacy, and public discourse to counter efforts to delegitimize Israel.

ACLI now reaches tens of thousands of pastors and Christian leaders who collectively represent millions of American believers, giving Christian support for Israel a clear public voice and cultural influence in the national conversation.

THE MATURITY OF MODERN CHRISTIAN ZIONISM

Together with initiatives like ACLI, the ICEJ reflects the maturity of modern Christian Zionism—a broad-based and organized movement rooted in Scripture that connects advocacy with practical action. It's a movement that goes beyond sympathy or symbolic support—Christian Zionism is a commitment to love and bless the Jewish people whom God set apart to bring glory to His name as commanded in Scripture (Isaiah 40:1) and to fight for Israel's right to exist, flourish, and defend itself in the land God set apart for them to further His purposes.

YOUR INVITATION

Modern Christian Zionists feel a moral and spiritual imperative to stand with Israel and cast their lot with the Jewish people. We invite you to join our efforts. We have much to do to combat rising antisemitism and reach our generation with the truth of God's Word.

Get involved at: www.icejusa.org/getinvolved

CONCLUSION

Christian Zionism is a biblical conviction rooted deeply in the unfailing character of God. From the beginning of Genesis to the prophets and writings and on to the Gospels and Paul's and Peter's epistles, the Bible affirms God's enduring purposes for the Jewish people and the significance of the land in His grand plan of redemption.

Unlike some who claim Christian Zionism is new, it is entrenched in Christianity's Jewish roots and God's plan for Israel and the nations. He is bringing redemption! But it is coming from an unlikely source: a specific people set apart for His purposes. This coming restoration is solely to glorify Him and His faithfulness to His word and His promises.

For Christians, this is not about adopting a particular political stance. Instead, it's about how we read the Bible. *Are we reading Scripture on its own terms and allowing it to shape our theology, attitudes, actions, and ultimately, our worldview?* Any other way allows incorrect theology to seep in.

Christian Zionism is a call to recognize God's hand at work in history, amid complexity and controversy.

It's a call to stand against antisemitism and pray for the peace of Jerusalem (Psalm 122:6).

It's a call to boldly confront lies, push back against silence, and proclaim the truth of God's Word amid loud voices that speak otherwise.

Most importantly, it's a call to have a posture of humility

and love toward the Jewish people as we continue to mend that relationship—knowing God will use it as a witness to His glory.

God is moving His purposes forward, and as He continues to gather His people from all the earth to the beautiful land set apart for His redemptive plan to come to pass. Christian Zionism invites the church to respond—not with fear or confusion but with faith, gratitude, and obedience to the One who keeps His covenant forever.

Hear the word of the Lord, O nations, and declare it in the isles afar off, and say, "He who scattered Israel will gather him, and keep him as a shepherd does his flock."
— Jeremiah 31:10

▪▮▪ RECOMMENDED READING ▪▮▪

BOOKS

Lewis, Donald M. *A Short History of Christian Zionism: From the Reformation to the Twenty-First Century.* Downers Grove, IL: InterVarsity Press, 2021.

McDermott, Gerald. *Israel Matters.* Grand Rapids, MI: Brazos Press, a division of Baker Book Publishing, 2017.

——. *The New Christian Zionism: Fresh Perspectives on Israel & the Land.* Downers Grove, IL: InterVarsity Press Academic, 2016.

BOOKLETS

Michael, Susan. *Antisemitism: What Every Christian Needs to Know and How to Counter It.* Murfreesboro, TN: Embassy Publishers, 2023.

Michael, Susan and Karen Engle. *Replacement Theology: What It Is and Why It Matters.* Murfreesboro, TN: Embassy Publishers, 2024.

Hedding, Malcolm. *The Basis of Christian Support for Israel. Biblical Zionism Series, Part 1.* International Christian Embassy Jerusalem–USA, Inc., 2004.

——. *The Great Covenants of the Bible: Biblical Zionism Series 3.* International Christian Embassy Jerusalem-USA, Inc., 2005, https://store.icejusa.org/products/the-great-covenants-of-the-bible

ARTICLES

Buehler, Juergen. "Healing the Rift: 1700 Years After the Nicaea Council." *ICEJ USA*, May 17, 2025. https://icejusa.org/2025/05/17/healing-the-rift-1700-years-after-the-nicaea-council/

———. "Israel and the Church: A Coming Reformation." *ICEJ USA*, September 24, 2024. https://icejusa.org/2024/09/24/israel-and-the-church-a-coming-reformation/

Hedding, Malcolm. "Israel and the Charge of Apartheid." *ICEJ*, accessed January 5, 2026. https://www.icej.org/understand-israel/israel-updates/israel-and-the-charge-of-apartheid/

———. "What Is Christian Zionism?" *Charisma Magazine Online*, March 26, 2010. https://mycharisma.com/news/what-is-christian-zionism2/

Michael, Susan. "Across the Israel Divide." *ICEJ USA*, September 19, 2016. https://icejusa.org/2016/09/19/across-the-israel-divide/

———. "Did the Jews Steal the Palestinians' Land?" *ICEJ USA*, May 4, 2017. https://icejusa.org/2017/05/04/did-the-jews-steal-the-palestinians-land/

———. "Is It Anti-Arab to Be Pro-Israel?" *ICEJ USA*, September 20, 2016. https://icejusa.org/2016/09/20/is-it-anti-arab-to-be-pro-israel/

———. "Was Israel Founded on Stolen Land?" *ICEJ USA*, April 5, 2022. https://icejusa.org/2022/04/05/was-israel-founded-on-stolen-arab-land/

Miller, Tricia. "No, Tucker, Christian Zionism Is NOT Christian Heresy!" *Israel365News*, November 5, 2025. https://israel365news.com/413777/no-tucker-christian-zionism-is-not-christian-heresy/

Parsons, David. "The Promise of Rest: God's Enduring Covenant with Israel." *International Christian Embassy Jerusalem (ICEJ) Blog*, January 4, 2025. https://www.icej.org/blog/the-promise-of-rest-gods-enduring-covenant-with-israel/

▮▯ FREE RESOURCES ▯▮

Request your FREE downloadable resource *5 Reasons Christians Should Support Israel*—and share it with family and friends. This full-color resource includes vibrant pictures and 5 reasons why we should support, bless, and stand with God's chosen people, the Jews. You'll also be alerted when we release a new book, online course, or other educational tools!

GET YOUR FREE RESOURCE TODAY
www.icejusa.org/5-reasons-christians-should-support-israel
or scan the QR code below

LEARN ABOUT RESOURCES
by ICEJ USA President Dr. Susan Michael at:
www.susanmichael.com

LEARN MORE ABOUT THE MINISTRY
of the International Christian Embassy Jerusalem at:
www.icejusa.org

FOLLOW US ON
www.facebook.com/icejusa
www.instagram.com/icejusaofficial/#
www.youtube.com/@ICEJUSAOFFICIAL

LEARN MORE ABOUT
ICEJ U online courses, books, and podcasts at: www.iceju.org

CONTACT US AT
www.icejusa.org

GET INVOLVED AT
www.icejusa.org/getinvolved

■■■ ABOUT THE AUTHOR

DR. SUSAN MICHAEL

For more than 40 years, Dr. Susan Michael has pioneered the development of the International Christian Embassy Jerusalem (ICEJ) in the United States and internationally. She currently serves as the ministry's USA President and is a member of the ICEJ's international board of directors.

Susan's involvement with the ICEJ began as a graduate student at Jerusalem University College in 1980, the same year the Christian Embassy was first established. Upon completing her master's degree in Judeo-Christian Studies, she returned from Israel with a heart to further the Embassy's mission among fellow Americans. After a season assisting the ministry's international leadership in hosting a series of high-profile pro-Israel conferences across the United States, she was asked to head up the ICEJ's USA Branch.

In addition to a master's degree in Judeo-Christian Studies, she holds a bachelor's degree in theology from Oral Roberts University and was awarded an Honorary Doctorate of Laws by Piedmont International University in 2018. Susan is an author, gifted teacher, and international speaker. She is often called upon to address complex and sensitive issues such as antisemitism, Islam, Jewish-Christian relations, and current events in the Middle East to a diverse range of audiences. Her experience working with Arabs, Jews, and Christians from many national and denominational backgrounds has equipped her to handle delicate topics central to an understanding of Israel with extraordinary clarity and grace.

In recent years she has produced several educational

tools to enable other Christians to do the same, including the IsraelAnswers.com website, a series of highly accessible educational seminars, online courses at ICEJ U, course curricula for Christian colleges, and Embassy Publishers. Susan has built the USA Branch of the ICEJ into a scripturally sound and reputable ministry, evidenced in its leadership of one of the strongest networks of Evangelical leaders in America—the American Christian Leaders for Israel (ACLI).

Susan is the author of *Encounter the 3D Bible: How to Read the Bible So It Comes to Life, Antisemitism: What Every Christian Needs to Know and How to Counter It,* and the award-winning *Every Generation's Story: 75 Years of American Christian Engagement with Israel.*

— ABOUT EMBASSY PUBLISHERS —

Embassy Publishers is the publishing arm of the International Christian Embassy Jerusalem designed to introduce the Christian reader to the biblical significance of Israel and the Jewish people, the history of antisemitism, Jewish-Christian relations, the modern State of Israel, and Christian engagement with Israel.

— ABOUT THE ICEJ —

The International Christian Embassy Jerusalem was established in 1980 in recognition of the biblical significance of all of Jerusalem and its unique connection with the Jewish people. Today, it represents millions of Christians, churches, and denominations to the nation and people of Israel. We recognize in the restoration of the State of Israel God's faithfulness to keep His ancient covenant with the Jewish people.

Our goal is to stand with Israel in support and friendship, equip and teach the worldwide church regarding God's purposes with Israel and the nations of the Middle East, be an active voice of reconciliation between Jews, Christians, and Arabs, and support the churches and congregations in the Holy Land. From its head offices in Jerusalem, the ICEJ reaches out to more than 170 countries worldwide, with branch offices and representation in over 90 nations.

CONTACT US
International Christian Embassy Jerusalem – USA, Inc.
PO Box 332974, Murfreesboro, TN 37133-2974
Tel: (615) 895-9830 • www.icejusa.org

Made in the USA
Monee, IL
26 January 2026

42514313R00030